CULTURAL CONTRIBUTIONS FROM

LATIN AMERICA

TORTILLAS, COLOR TV, AND MORE

GREAT CULTURES,
GREAT IDEAS

MADELINE TYLER

PowerKiDS
press

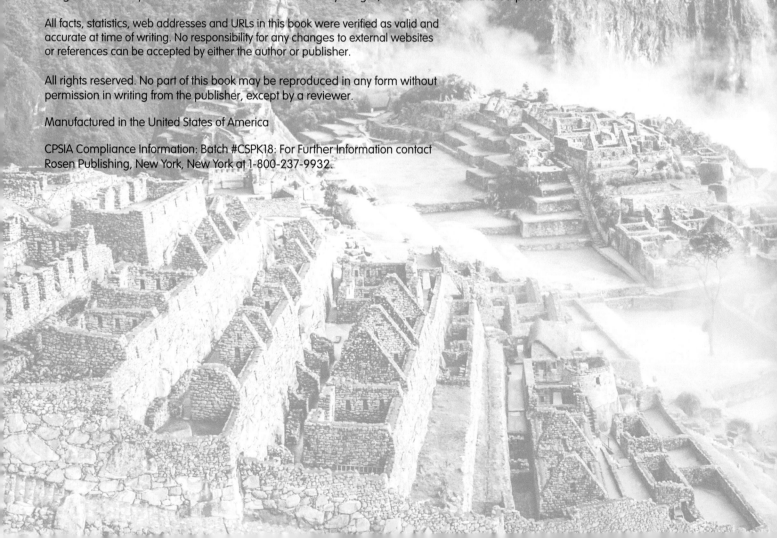

Published in 2019 by The Rosen Publishing Group, Inc.
29 East 21st Street, New York, NY 10010

Cataloging-in-Publication Data

Names: Tyler, Madeline.
Title: Cultural contributions from Latin America: tortillas, color TV, and more / Madeline Tyler.
Description: New York : PowerKids Press, 2019. | Series: Great cultures, great ideas | Includes glossary and index.
Identifiers: LCCN ISBN 9781538338308 (pbk.) | ISBN 9781538338292 (library bound) | ISBN 9781538338315 (6 pack)
Subjects: LCSH: Latin America--Social life and customs--Juvenile literature. | Latin America--Intellectual life--Juvenile literature.
Classification: LCC F1408.3 T954 2019 | DDC 980--dc23

Written by: Madeline Tyler
Edited by: Kirsty Holmes
Designed by: Matt Rumbelow

Photo credits
Abbreviations: l-left, r-right, b-bottom, t-top, c-center, m-middle.

Front Cover – Stocksnapper, stockcreations, Hong Vo, Mile Atanasov, dubassy, Chuck Rausin, Valentyn Volkov, 3DMAVR, Scorpp, Amr Hassanein, maramorosz, Pro3DArtt, 2 – Volodymyr Burdiak, 4 – stocker1970, Jakkarin Apikornrat, AJP, Memory Stockphoto, piyaphong, 5 – Sergey Clocikov, AJ Frames, Sata Production, 6 – I am Corona, hxdyl, leungchopan, 7 – Maximumvector, charnsitr, maxfoto.shutter, www.petrovvladimir.ru, 8 – Ad_hominem, fredex, Christian Vinces. 9/10 – Pyty, Rainer Lesniewski, lazyllama. 12/13 – Lukiyanova Natalia frenta, Dmitry Polonskiy, virtu studio, Chiociolla, Igor Kovalchuk. 14/15 – David Ionut, vkilikov, fotoliza, FeyginFoto. 16/17 – Jujubier, Bildagentur Zoonar GmbH, xstockerx, Facto Photo, Alice Nerr. 18/19 – Kateryna Kon, Gustavo Frazao, Dirk Ercken, Johnny Lye, pruit phatsrivong, vectorEps. 20/21 – lazyllama, Boris Medvedev, Aleksandar Grozdanovski, Clive Chilvers, Vibrant Pictures, LongJon. 22/23 – sunsinger, AGCuesta, Dina Julayeva, Kobby Dagan, WikiCommons. 24/25 – istetiana, Foodio, Ildi Papp, Kayo, Foodio, Joshua Resnick, Viktoria Petrova, tonfon, Elena Veselova, Janet Moore, Brent Hofacker, zoryanchik, Dream79. 26/27 – Julia Zharkova, Minerva Studio, Patchareephoto, Michael Drager, JORGE TERRE OLIVA, Sanit Fuangnakhon, James Steidl. 28/29 – CLIPAREA | Custom media, crystal light, Ozgur Guvenc. 30 – Kyselova Inna, Iakov Filimonov, Dmitrij Skorobogatov, Cheers Group.Lukiyanova, Natalia frenta.

Images are courtesy of Shutterstock.com. With thanks to Getty Images, Thinkstock Photo and iStockphoto.

All facts, statistics, web addresses and URLs in this book were verified as valid and accurate at time of writing. No responsibility for any changes to external websites or references can be accepted by either the author or publisher.

Manufactured in the United States of America

CPSIA Compliance Information: Batch #CSPK18: For Further Information contact Rosen Publishing, New York, New York at 1-800-237-9932.

CONTENTS

Words that look like **this** are explained in the glossary on page 31.

WHAT IS CULTURE?

If you were to travel around the world, visiting lots of countries on the way, you would probably notice that certain things around you would not be the same as they are at home. The countries and places you visit, and the people you meet, would have different languages, customs, and ways of doing things. The food might be different, the way people dress might be different, and even the laws and rules might be different to what you know at home. All of these things, when put together, make up what we call the culture of a place.

A HOUSE IN CHINA MIGHT LOOK VERY DIFFERENT THAN ONE IN THE UK!

WHAT MAKES UP A CULTURE?

Shared ideas and traditions that make up a culture can include:

LAWS	BELIEFS	SCHOOLS
FOOD	CEREMONIES	SPECIAL BUILDINGS
LEADERS	HOLIDAYS	HOSPITALS
SYMBOLS	FAMILIES	ENTERTAINMENT

A culture can also be shared by a group of people who might not live near each other, but who share a way of life. People who like the same music or hobbies can share a culture. People who all belong to the same religion can be said to share a culture, no matter where they live.

BEAUTIFUL HENNA TATTOOS ARE PART OF INDIAN CULTURE. MANY INDIAN BRIDES AROUND THE WORLD PRACTICE THIS CULTURAL TRADITION.

DIFFERENT CULTURES GREET EACH OTHER IN DIFFERENT WAYS – A HANDSHAKE, A BOW, OR EVEN A KISS!

Our culture is a big part of our identity. Having a distinctive culture is what makes places or people unique. Knowing you belong to a particular culture is a good feeling. It's nice to share our culture with other people. If we are in a culture we recognize, we understand what to do or how to act.

GLOBAL CULTURE

Even though every culture is different and has many things that make it unique, many cultures also have lots of things in common. We can learn a lot from other cultures, and share the things we know and like. In the past, when people started traveling and visiting other cultures, they began to swap and share their food, traditions, and knowledge. People started to adopt things from other cultures into their own. For example, British people see drinking tea as part of their cultural identity, but tea is originally from China and is also an important part of Japanese culture.

AFTERNOON TEA, WITH CAKES AND SANDWICHES, IS A TRADITIONAL PART OF ENGLISH CULTURE.

It is also really interesting to explore other cultures and discover new and exciting ways of doing things! We can share our ideas and learn new things when cultures meet.

TEA WAS ORIGINALLY FROM CHINA AND ORIGINATED DURING THE SHANG DYNASTY.

IN JAPAN, THE TEA CEREMONY IS AN IMPORTANT CULTURAL RITUAL.

MY CULTURE, YOUR CULTURE,, OUR CULTURE

Adopting ideas from other cultures can lead to really interesting results. Many cultures take inspiration from others and adapt and change their traditions and customs to make them their own. Putting two ideas from two different cultures together can produce new and exciting things. Did you know that a pizza in Italy will look very different from a pizza in the US? Italians introduced pizza, a traditional Italian dish, to the Americans living in the US. A traditional Italian pizza has a thin, crispy crust, and lots of tomato, but only a small amount of mozzarella cheese. An American pizza has a thick, fluffy base, is smothered in cheese, and can have lots of different toppings—meats, fish, even pineapple! Both cultures share a love for pizza, but each culture has their own way of doing things!

TRADITIONAL ITALIAN PIZZA

AMERICAN PIZZA

WHICH PIZZA DO YOU PREFER? ITALIAN, AMERICAN, OR MAYBE A SLICE OF EACH?

WHERE IS LATIN AMERICA?

Latin America is a large region made up of the continent of South America, Central America including Mexico, and the Caribbean Islands. Latin America can be found in the Western **Hemisphere** and is so large that it spans both the Northern and Southern hemispheres.

Mexico

Capital city: Mexico City

Population: 129,000,000 people

Size: 758,449 square miles (1,964,274 sq km)

Currency: Peso

Major Religion(s): Christianity

Main Language(s): Spanish

Colombia

Capital city: Bogota

Population: 49,000,000 people

Size: 440,831 square miles (1,141,667 sq km)

Currency: Peso

Major Religion(s): Christianity

Main Language(s): Spanish

Peru

Capital city: Lima

Population: 32,100,000 people

Size: 496,225 square miles (1,285,217 sq km)

Currency: Nuevo sol

Major religion(s): Christianity

Main language(s): Spanish, Quechua, Aymara

LIMA, PERU

Venezuela

Capital city: Caracas

Population: 32,000,000 people

Size: 340,561 square miles
(882,049 sq km)

Currency: Bolivar

Major Religion(s): Christianity

Main Language(s): Spanish,
Indigenous Languages

Brazil

Capital city: Brasilia

Population: 209,400,000 people

Size: 3,300,000 square miles
(8,546,961 sq km)

Currency: Real

Major Religion(s): Christianity

Main Language(s): Portuguese

Argentina

Capital city: Buenos Aires

Population: 44,300,000 people

Size: 1,100,000 square miles
(2,848,987 sq km)

Currency: Peso

Major Religion(s): Christianity

Main Language(s): Spanish

CARIBBEAN ISLANDS

The Caribbean Islands are a group of islands in the Caribbean Sea to the east of Mexico. There are around 7,000 different islands in the Caribbean. Some are quite big and have millions of people living on them, while others are tiny and have very few **inhabitants**, if any! Caribbean culture is very diverse and has been influenced by African, European, and Native American cultures.

Cuba

Capital city: Havana

Population: 11,400,000 people

Size: 42,803 square miles (110,859 sq km)

Currency: Cuban Peso

Major Religion(s): Christianity

Main Language(s): Spanish

Jamaica

Capital city: Kingston

Population: 2,885,000 people

Size: 4,243 square miles (10,989 sq km)

Currency: Jamaican Dollar

Major Religion(s): Christianity

Main Language(s): English, English patois

JAMAICA AT THE OLYMPICS

If you have ever watched the **Olympic Games**, you may have noticed that Jamaica is very successful in one sport in particular: athletics. Athletics is made up of various events including short-distance **sprint** races, long-distance races, the long jump, high jump, and javelin throw. One very successful Jamaican Olympic athlete is Usain Bolt.

Born:	Sherwood Content, Jamaica
Competed:	4 Olympic Games
Medals:	8 Gold Medals
Achievements:	8 World Records
	Fastest 100 meters (m)
	Fastest 200 m
	Fastest 4x100 m relay

Haiti

Capital city: Port-au-Prince

Population: 10,980,000 people

Size: 10,714 square miles (27,749 sq km)

Currency: Gourde

Major Religion(s): Christianity

Main Language(s): Creole, French

Dominican Republic

Capital city: Santo Domingo

Population: 10,760,000 people

Size: 18,704 square miles (48,072 sq km)

Currency: Dominican Peso

Major Religion(s): Christianity

Main Language(s): Spanish

AZTECS AND MAYA

The Aztecs were a group of people who lived in Mexico during the 14th century. They ruled a large **empire** called the Aztec Empire in Central America. The Aztecs and other similar civilizations, such as the Maya, are well known for building great pyramid temples. One example is the Templo Mayor, a huge pyramid in the centre of Tenochtitlan, the Aztec capital. Templo Mayor was built almost 600 years ago and was an important religious site in the Aztec Empire.

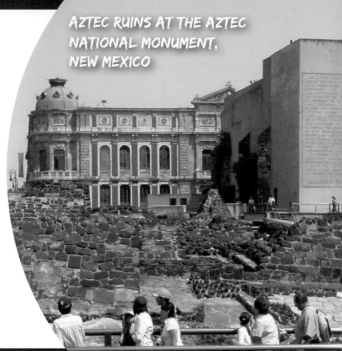

AZTEC RUINS AT THE AZTEC NATIONAL MONUMENT, NEW MEXICO

THE TEMPLO MAYOR IS NOW IN RUINS IN THE CENTER OF MEXICO CITY.

One of the most recognizable pyramids in Latin America is the Pyramid of Kukulcan. The Pyramid of Kukulcan is also called El Castillo. It is a large pyramid in the ancient Maya city of Chichen Itza. It is around 900 years old and would have been used for religious ceremonies and **sacrifices**. As the Maya civilization existed thousands of years before the Aztec Empire, it is likely that the Aztec people took inspiration from Maya **architecture** like El Castillo.

EL CASTILLO IS 79 FEET TALL!

FOODS FROM THE PAST

POPCORN

It was not a movie snack yet, and it probably wasn't sweetened or salted, but popcorn dates back over 6,000 years to a time before even the Maya civilization. The first people to grow corn to eat were the inhabitants of ancient Mexico around 9,000 years ago, and it was first "popped" 3,000 years later. Microwave ovens had not been invented yet, so people had to roast the cob over a fire to make the popcorn.

CORN ON
THE COB

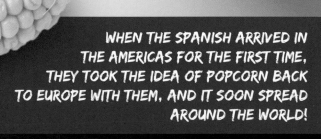

WHEN THE SPANISH ARRIVED IN THE AMERICAS FOR THE FIRST TIME, THEY TOOK THE IDEA OF POPCORN BACK TO EUROPE WITH THEM, AND IT SOON SPREAD AROUND THE WORLD!

HOT CHOCOLATE

Another invention we can thank the Aztecs for is hot chocolate. The Aztecs used to drink a spicy hot chocolate made from cacao beans, corn flour, water, and chilies. People from Spain added sugar, and the drink soon evolved into the hot chocolate we know and love.

THE AZTECS CALLED THEIR DRINK XOCOLATL (SAY: SHO-KO-LA-TUL), WHICH MEANS "BITTER WATER."

THE INCA

The Inca Empire was founded around AD 1200 and was ruled by one leader. The Inca Empire was huge, covering 9,065 miles (14,585 km) of land along the west coast of South America. Many of the Inca people settled high up in the Andes mountains, much higher than any other civilization. One famous Inca settlement site is Machu Picchu in present-day Peru.

MACHU PICCHU AND HUAYNA PICCHU ARE TWO MOUNTAINS THAT SURROUND THE MACHU PICCHU SITE.

"MACHU PICCHU" MEANS "OLD MOUNTAIN" IN THE QUECHUA LANGUAGE THAT WAS USED BY THE INCAS. MACHU PICCHU IS NAMED AFTER THE NEARBY MOUNTAIN WITH THE SAME NAME.

Machu Picchu is an ancient Inca town high in the Andes that now lays in ruins. Machu Picchu is made up of houses, farming areas, communal buildings like temples, and a cemetery. Many people believe that Machu Picchu was built as either a royal **retreat** or as a **sanctuary**. The area is a natural **fortress**, protected by the surrounding steep slopes of Machu Picchu and Huayna Picchu.

INCA LAMOIDS

Llamas and alpacas are closely related and are part of a group of animals from South America called lamoids. The first people to **domesticate** llamas and alpacas were the ancient civilizations living in the Andes mountains of Peru around 5,000 years ago. Llamas and alpacas are stronger than humans, so they were often bred to be used as pack animals. A pack animal is one that is used to carry heavy loads to help humans.

HOWEVER, THIS WAS NOT THE ONLY USE THE INCA FOUND FOR THE ANIMALS. THEY ALSO USED LLAMAS AND ALPACAS FOR THEIR WOOLLY COATS BY REMOVING AND WEAVING THE WOOL TO MAKE CLOTHING.

ALPACA WOOL IS OFTEN DYED BRIGHT COLORS AND MADE INTO SCARVES.

PERU IS THE LARGEST PRODUCER OF ALPACA WOOL, AND PRODUCTS ARE EXPORTED WORLDWIDE.

Alpaca wool is very soft, warm, strong, and lightweight. It is also rain and snow **resistant**, so it is the perfect material to make coats and other products like sleeping bags. In the Inca civilization, only royal or **noble** people could wear robes made from alpaca wool, but now anyone can.

MOUNTAINS AND WATERFALLS

THE ANDES MOUNTAINS

The Andes are a series of extremely high **mountain ranges** that run along the west coast of South America. The Andes is the longest stretch of mountains in the world and runs through Argentina, Chile, Colombia, Peru, Bolivia, Venezuela, and Ecuador!

THE HIGHEST MOUNTAIN IN THE ANDES IS MOUNT ACONCAGUA ON THE BORDER OF ARGENTINA AND CHILE. IT STANDS AT AN IMPRESSIVE 22,481 FEET (6,960 M) TALL!

SPECTACLED BEAR

The climate in the Andes is very extreme. Some parts are warm and rainy, while in other parts it is very cold and often snows. Animals, and even some people, live in these harsh conditions. The highest **altitude** that people have lived in the Andes is around 17,060 feet (5,200 m) above sea level – that is around 14 times higher than the Empire State Building in New York City!

Many different types of animals live in the Andes, including alpacas, llamas, guinea pigs, spectacled bears, yellow-tailed woolly monkeys, and chinchillas.

CHINCHILLA

YELLOW-TAILED WOOLLY MONKEY

GUINEA PIG

ANGEL FALLS

When water in a river flows off a rocky ledge, we call it a waterfall. Some waterfalls are tall and narrow, like Angel Falls, and others are wider but much shorter, like Niagara Falls. Angel Falls is the highest waterfall in the world and is found in Venezuela.

DURING THE RAINY SEASON, THE WATERFALL SPLITS INTO TWO. DURING THE DRY SEASON THE WATER SOMETIMES EVAPORATES INTO MIST BEFORE IT REACHES THE BOTTOM!

THIS IS NIAGARA FALLS, WHICH IS FOUND ON THE BORDER BETWEEN CANADA AND THE US.

Angel Falls was discovered and made known to the world in the 1930s when an American adventurer called James Angel crashed his plane nearby. The waterfall was named after James Angel, and is now one of the most visited sites in Venezuela.

ANGEL FALLS IS 3,211 FEET (979 M) HIGH!
THIS IS 19 TIMES HIGHER THAN NIAGARA FALLS!

THE AMAZON

THE AMAZON RAINFOREST

Rainforests are a type of forest that is found in very warm places and receives a lot of rain. This rain helps the trees and plants to grow, providing a home and food to the many creatures that live there.

AROUND 500 INDIGENOUS TRIBES LIVE IN THE AMAZON RAINFOREST!

The largest rainforest in the world is the Amazon Rainforest, which spreads across Brazil, Ecuador, Venezuela, Suriname, Peru, Colombia, Bolivia, Guyana, and French Guinea. It covers 2,316,612 square miles (6,000,000 sq km). That's over twice as big as the whole country of India!

The Amazon Rainforest is so **biodiverse** that 10% of all the world's animal and plant species are found here. The Amazon Rainforest is important to the whole world, and not just the animals that live there. It is sometimes called the lungs of the Earth because it takes carbon dioxide out of the air and produces more than 20% of the world's oxygen.

POISON DART FROG

THE AMAZON RIVER

The Amazon River flows through the Amazon Rainforest and starts high up in the Andes mountains. It is 4,345 miles (6,990 km) long and flows through Peru, Bolivia, Venezuela, Colombia, Ecuador, and Brazil. The river is so long that its length is the same as the distance between Rome and New York City!

THE AMAZON RIVER IS THE WORLD'S LONGEST RIVER.

RED-BELLIED PIRANHA

The Amazon River is home to over 3,000 **species** of fish, and one type you may have heard of is the piranha. Piranhas have very strong jaws and sharp teeth, and can attack animals much larger than themselves. They are very fierce and quite scary to look at.

AMAZON RIVER DOLPHIN

The river is also home to the Amazon River dolphin, the largest species of dolphin that only lives in **freshwater**. They are sometimes called pink river dolphins, because some dolphins of this species have been known to become pink as they get older.

RIO DE JANEIRO

Carnivals are a type of celebration that can be found in cities all around the world. The most famous carnival is the Rio Carnival in Brazil.

The first carnival in Brazil was in 1723, but this was a very different type of carnival. People went into the streets and covered each other in water, food, and mud! In the 20th century, music, dance, and costumes became more important until it evolved into the street parade that we are familiar with today. Rio Carnival is a lively celebration full of brightly colored outfits, music, and dancing.

A CAIXA IS A SNARE DRUM. IT MAKES A RATTLING SOUND.

THE SURDO IS A LARGE DRUM THAT IS THE HEARTBEAT OF THE SAMBA.

SAMBA

Samba is mixture of music, song, and dance, and was brought to Brazil from Africa in the 19th century. It is enjoyed by people of all ages, rich and poor, and is central to Rio Carnival.

Drums are important to samba music because they set the beat for the dance. The drums section of a samba band is called the *bateria* and is made up of lots of different types of drums.

LONDON

Notting Hill Carnival is a carnival in London, UK, that celebrates African and Caribbean life and culture. The first Notting Hill Carnival was in 1966 and began as a street party for the children living nearby. The Russ Henderson Steel Band, a steel pan band who were performing at the party, started walking round the streets. More and more people joined them, and the procession grew and grew.

Notting Hill Carnival is a much larger event now. There are now around 10 steel pan bands instead of just one, as well as thousands of other musicians and performers. You can find musical performances, food stalls, and thousands of costumes at the carnival.

THIS IS A STEEL PAN BAND COMPETING IN THE PANORAMA STEEL BAND COMPETITION IN LONDON.

THERE ARE UP TO TWO MILLION PEOPLE AT NOTTING HILL CARNIVAL EVERY YEAR, MAKING IT THE SECOND LARGEST CARNIVAL IN THE WORLD AFTER RIO CARNIVAL.

NOTTING HILL CARNIVAL IS THE LARGEST STREET FESTIVAL IN EUROPE!

DÍA DE LOS MUERTOS

Día de los Muertos is a Mexican festival that started thousands of years ago in the ancient civilizations of Latin America. The Aztec and **Toltec** people did not believe in **mourning** the dead, as they saw death as a natural part of life. Instead, they wanted to celebrate the lives of the people who had died and keep them alive in people's memory.

DÍA DE LOS MUERTOS MEANS "DAY OF THE DEAD" IN SPANISH.

THIS IS A DÍA DE LOS MUERTOS ALTAR.

The Día de los Muertos celebrations take place on the 1st and 2nd of November. People from Mexico believe that the spirits of their dead friends and family return to Earth during this time to celebrate with them. An important tradition of Día de los Muertos is the altar, or ofrenda, which is built to welcome spirits back to Earth. The altar is made in people's homes and contains food, water, family photos, flowers, and candles.

Celebrations include wearing face paint and costumes, having street parades and parties, and doing lots of singing and dancing.

CALAVERA CATRINA

This popular image of a skeleton has become the symbol of Día de los Muertos, but it was created a lot more recently than the festival. It is called "calavera Catrina" and was first drawn by a Mexican artist called José Guadalupe Posada in the 20th century.

THE FIRST "CALAVERA CATRINA."

Nowadays it is very common to dress up as a skeleton for Día de los Muertos and to have your face painted in the style of calavera Catrina. The design is now popular around the world. It is used in decorations, too.

Día de los Muertos has become so well known around the world that Disney Pixar has even made a film based on the festival! *Coco* is set in Mexico during Día de los Muertos. It is about a Mexican boy and the skeletons of his **ancestors**.

THIS IS A PHOTO OF A DÍA DE LOS MUERTOS CARNIVAL IN AGUASCALIENTES, MEXICO.

CARIBBEAN

Caribbean **cuisine** is a **fusion** of all the different people and cultures that have passed through and lived in the region in the past. Traditional recipes from the indigenous people of the islands have evolved through European, East Asian, African, and Indian influences to create the Caribbean cuisine of today.

Jerk chicken is a very popular dish from Jamaica. It involves rubbing the chicken with a mixture of different spices and peppers, and cooking it slowly over wood from the allspice tree.

This could have come from the **Arawak people** in Jamaica during the 18th century. They used salt, peppers, and spices to **preserve** the wild boar meat they caught, and then cooked it over a fire.

The Cuban sandwich is a popular lunch in both Cuba and Florida. It contains sliced pork, ham brought to Cuba from Spain, cheese, dill pickles, and mustard.

Riz collé aux pois, which is rice with kidney beans, is a popular dish in Haiti. It is considered their national dish.

Goat stew is popular in the Caribbean and in many countries in Africa.

MEXICAN

"Tex-Mex" is a mixture of North American and Mexican cuisines. The cuisine is inspired by Mexican dishes and is popular in the US and the UK. The dishes are typically spicy and use lots of cheese, beans, peppers, meat, and spices.

Nachos are a Tex-Mex dish from northern Mexico. They are crispy tortilla chips covered in cheese and other toppings including salsa, sour cream, guacamole, and jalapeño peppers. Sometimes they even have beef or chicken on top!

A burrito is made by filling a soft tortilla with meat and refried beans, and wrapping it up. Although burritos are Mexican, it is the Tex-Mex style burritos that added extra fillings like rice, salsa, cheese, and vegetables.

Chili con carne means "chili with meat." It is a spicy dish made with beef, tomatoes, chili peppers, and kidney beans.

THE TERM "TEX-MEX" COMES FROM ADDING TWO WORDS TOGETHER — "TEXAS" AND "MEXICO"!

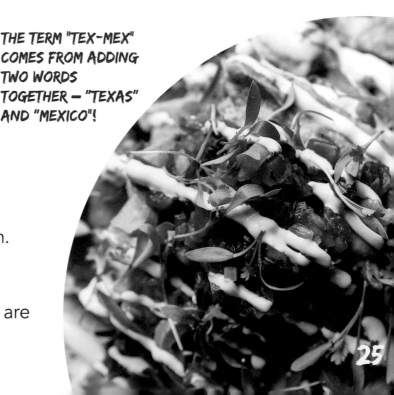

The Aztecs made a flat bread from corn. They called this food *tlaxcali*. Spanish invaders gave the bread a different name - "tortilla." Corn and flour tortillas are a huge part of Latin American cuisine.

COLOR TELEVISION

Can you imagine turning on the television to watch your favorite show, but everything is in black and white with no color? This is what people had to do before color television was invented around 70 years ago. Everything on the television would have looked black, white, or grey.

Guillermo González Camarena was a very successful Mexican inventor who introduced color television to Mexico. Camarena invented a device to convert black and white television into color television. In 1963, Camarena made the first ever color broadcast in Mexico.

Camarena also developed a cheaper version of color television called Simplified Bicolour System so that everyone in Mexico could afford to use it.

GUILLERMO GONZÁLEZ CAMARENA IS VERY CELEBRATED IN MEXICO. HIS BIRTHDAY, THE 17TH OF FEBRUARY, 1917, IS NOW CALLED "DAY OF THE INVENTOR."

BALLPOINT PEN

Ballpoint pens are one of the most popular writing tools in the world. Before the ballpoint pen, people used something called a fountain pen. Fountain pens used a type of ink that took a long time to dry and would smudge across the page very easily.

A FOUNTAIN PEN

László Bíró was a Hungarian journalist who lived in Argentina for much of his life. Bíró wanted to create a pen that used fast-drying ink and would not smudge as much as a fountain pen.

Bíró created his first ballpoint pen in 1931 and, in 1943, he formed a company in Argentina to **manufacture** his invention.

He named his invention the "Eterpen," but it is now referred to as a "Birome" in Argentina, a biro in the UK, and a ballpoint pen in the US and beyond.

The ballpoint pen has a tiny ball in its point. The ball is coated with ink and moves when it touches the paper.

IN THE UNITED KINGDOM, PEOPLE CALL A BALLPOINT PEN A BIRO. LOOK AT THE INVENTOR'S LAST NAME AND SEE IF YOU CAN GUESS WHY!

STENTS

WHAT IS A STENT?

A stent is a small tube made from a wire mesh. Stents are put inside weak arteries in a person's body to make the arteries stronger and to help them heal. Arteries are a type of **blood vessel** that carry blood from the heart to the rest of the body.

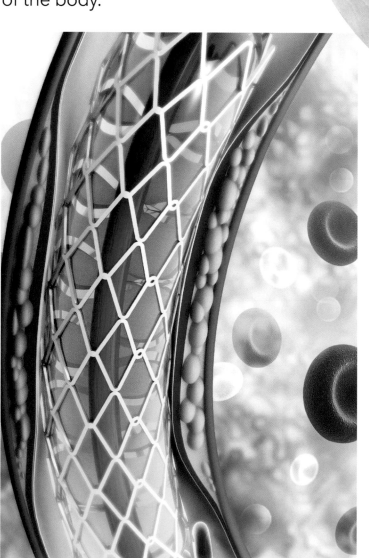

In 1978, an Argentinian doctor called Julio Palmaz came up with an idea to create something that could hold arteries open to help patients with heart problems. Palmaz developed his idea for the stent and created lots of **prototypes**. They were a success, and Palmaz put a stent into a patient for the first time in 1987. Stents are now used in two million patients every year.

STENTS ARE COLLAPSIBLE, BUT THEY HOLD THEIR SHAPE AND REMAIN RIGID ONCE THEY ARE FULLY EXPANDED.

ARTIFICIAL HEARTS

WHAT IS AN ARTIFICIAL HEART?

Sometimes people's hearts do not work very well and they must be replaced. Most people who need a new heart have a heart transplant operation where they receive a new heart from an organ donor. A small number of people receive an artificial, or mechanical, heart.

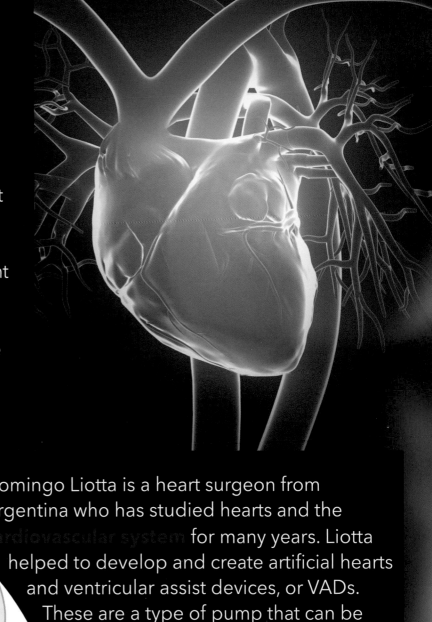

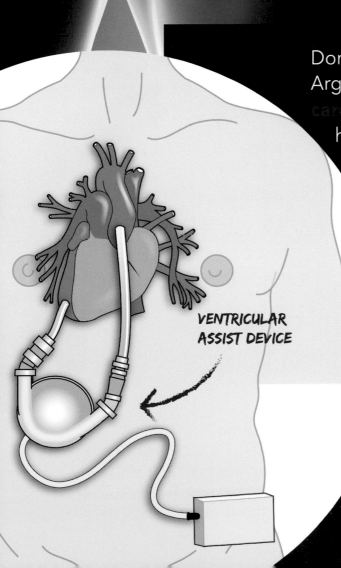

VENTRICULAR ASSIST DEVICE

Domingo Liotta is a heart surgeon from Argentina who has studied hearts and the cardiovascular system for many years. Liotta helped to develop and create artificial hearts and ventricular assist devices, or VADs. These are a type of pump that can be attached to someone's heart to help it pump more blood around the body. Liotta has helped to create VADs and total artificial hearts. VADs usually only replace one ventricle of the heart, but a total artificial heart replaces both the left ventricle and the right. Liotta helped to create one of the first total artificial hearts. This heart was successfully transplanted into a patient in 1969.

LANGUAGE

Nahuatl is a group of languages that were spoken by the Aztec people hundreds of years ago. More than a million people still speak Nahuatl, and many words are now used in the English language today. Can you match the English word with the Nahuatl word it came from?

Cacao	Tomatl
Coyote	Ōcēlōtl
Avocado	Xalapan
Tomato	Chīlli Pōctli
Chili	Āhuacamōlli
Ocelot	Chian
Chipotle	Xahcalli
Guacamole	Cacahuatl
Chia	Chīlli
Shack	Xocolatl
Chocolate	Mexihco
Mexico	Aztecatl
Aztec	Coyōtl
Jalapeño	Āhuacatl

Answers: Cacao = Cacahuatl, Coyote = Coyōtl, Avocado = Āhuacatl, Tomato = Tomatl, Chili = Chīlli, Ocelot = Ōcēlōtl, Chipotle = Chīlli Pōctli, Guacamole = Āhuacamōlli, Chia = Chian, Shack = Xahcalli, Chocolate = Xocolatl, Mexico = Mexihco, Aztec = Aztecatl, Jalapeño = Xalapan

GLOSSARY

altitude	the height of an object in relation to sea level or ground level
ancestors	persons from whom one is descended, such as a great-grandparent
Arawak people	a group of indigenous people who lived in South America and the Caribbean
architecture	style or way of building
biodiverse	when an area has lots of different types of animals or plants
blood vessel	tubes in the body through which blood flows
cardiovascular system	system in the body that circulates blood around the body
collapsible	can be collapsed down into a smaller size
cuisine	a style of cooking
domesticate	tame an animal so that it can be kept by humans
empire	a group of countries or nations under one ruler
evaporates	turns from liquid into a gas or vapor
fortress	a large, well-protected building
freshwater	water that is not salty and doesn't come from the sea
fusion	a mixture
hemisphere	a section of the Earth, either Northern, Southern, Eastern, or Western
indigenous	originating or naturally found in a particular place
inhabitants	people who live in a particular place
manufacture	to make a large quantity of something
mountain ranges	groups of connected mountains
mourning	acting or feeling very sad because someone has died
noble	when someone has a high rank or title
Olympic Games	an event held every four years in which athletes compete in various sports
organ donor	someone who donates organs from their body either before or after they die
preserve	to make something last a long time
prototypes	the original models of something that can be changed and developed later on
resistant	repels and does not feel the effect
retreat	a quiet area or building for resting and thinking
sacrifices	when an animal or person is killed and offered to a god or gods
sanctuary	a holy or sacred place
species	a group of very similar animals or plants that are capable of producing young together
sprint	to run as fast as you can
Toltec	a group of indigenous people who lived in Mexico before the Aztecs
ventricle	a section of the heart that pumps blood to the lungs and through the body

INDEX